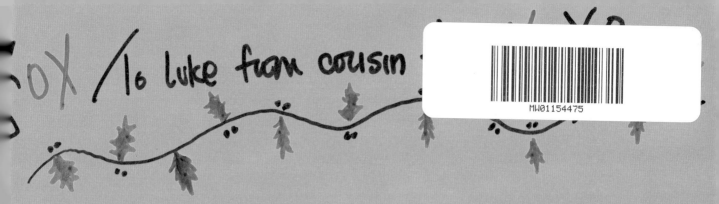

To luke from cousin

www.mascotbooks.com

Hello, Pounce

©2021 Donna Pasternak & Dr. Hope Longwell-Grice

For more information, please contact:
Mascot Books
620 Herndon Parkway, Suite 320
Herndon, VA 20170
info@mascotbooks.com

CPSIA Code: PRT0121A
ISBN-13: 978-1-62086-390-9

Printed in the United States

Hello, POUNCE

WRITTEN BY DR. DONNA PASTERNAK
& DR. HOPE LONGWELL-GRICE

ILLUSTRATED BY AGUS PRAJOGO

UNIVERSITY OF WISCONSIN
UWM
MILWAUKEE

It was a crisp, fall morning at the University of Wisconsin-Milwaukee when Pounce, the university's friendly panther mascot, woke up early in his room in Sandburg Hall.

The sun wasn't even up yet, so Pounce thought, *If I hurry, I can watch the sunrise from Bradford Beach*. Pounce's roommate was still fast asleep when Pounce quietly left their room, got on his bike, and was on his way.

When Pounce got to the beach, he walked over to the surf and sat on the cool sand. The sun rose slowly over Lake Michigan, its rays spreading over the calm water.

Look at all the oranges and yellows! thought Pounce as he buried his paws in the sand.

Just as he was thinking how happy he was that he woke up early, he heard, **"Hello, Pounce!"**

Pounce turned to see some of his friends who were students from the School of Freshwater Sciences. "Hello!" he replied as he walked toward them.

"We're about to take UWM's boat, the *Neeskay*, onto Lake Michigan. Would you like to join us and learn about freshwater science?"

"Sure!" replied Pounce.

Pounce spent a few sun-filled hours
learning about creatures and plants that
live deep underwater in Lake Michigan.
He even waved to a large-mouth bass
swimming by while the students operated a
300-pound sea robot!

Back at the shore, Pounce saw some friends building sandcastles on the beach for the annual contest at UWM's School of Architecture & Urban Planning.

"Hello, Pounce!" they called out. **"Come help us, please!"**

Pounce added the UWM flag to the tallest sandcastle as all his friends cheered. He hoped it would help them win the contest.

With the sun high in the sky, Pounce decided to enjoy the cool shade of UWM's Downer Woods. As he biked over, he noticed a group of students getting ready to take a hike. What a great opportunity to make new friends and get some exercise!

Pounce and his new friends made sure to leave the woods exactly as they found them.

What a wonderful walk, Pounce thought, but it was time to go to the Golda Meir Library and discover new books. He waved farewell to his hiking friends, and off he went.

PLEASE
DON'T
LITTER

Pounce arrived at the Golda Meir Library and was greeted with a hearty **"Hello, Pounce!"** from the head librarian. "Let's get to work learning how to find new information!"

"That sounds great!" said Pounce.

Pounce saw students enjoying fresh coffee at the Grind and discussing their homework in study groups. He saw rare books in the display cases on his way to a computer to learn the online library system.

Soon it was noon, and Pounce was hungry! After all the biking, hiking, and learning he had done, it was time to eat lunch.

Pounce made his way to the UWM Student Union and picked out a healthy meal: a turkey and cheese sandwich, an apple, and a carton of milk. He was looking for a place to sit when more friends yelled, **"Hello, Pounce! Come sit with us!"**

Pounce had a great time eating lunch with his friends.

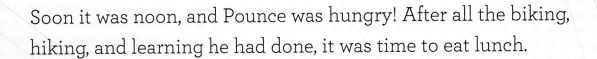

After lunch, Pounce was ready to play a game so he stopped by the UWM Panther Arena where the men's basketball team was practicing for their game tomorrow.

"Hello, Pounce!" they called while dribbling up and down the court.

"Can I take a shot?" Pounce asked.

"Sure! Join us!" they replied.

After practice, it was time for Pounce's art class. He loved painting!

Pounce dipped his paw into the gold paint and added his print to the canvas the class was working on together. **"Go Panthers!"** he and his classmates cheered.

Pounce's final stop for the day was the Manfred Olson Planetarium, where he arrived in time for a show about stars. When the students saw him, they yelled, **"Hello, Pounce!"**

Pounce learned about star constellations and was amazed by the wonders of outer space. Spotting a shooting star, he made a wish for another great day!

As soon as he returned to Sandburg Hall, Pounce changed into his pajamas and got ready for bed. It was time to call it a night after learning about freshwater sciences, the environment, the library, Milwaukee basketball, art, and outer space. He couldn't wait to dream about all the amazing things he had done.

Goodnight, Pounce!

About the Authors

Donna L. Pasternak is Professor of English Education and Director of the UWM Writing Project in the School of Education at the University of Wisconsin-Milwaukee. A certified English teacher who has taught middle and high school students in the United States, Norway, and Ecuador, she hopes you enjoy learning about UWM through Pounce's adventures and looks forward to seeing you on campus in the future.

Hope Longwell-Grice is the Associate Dean for Academic Affairs in the School of Education at the University of Wisconsin – Milwaukee. She is a certified Montessori Teacher who has taught children from ages 18 months through adulthood. This is Hope's first children's book. She hopes that you enjoy the adventures of Pounce. She also hopes that you will meet Pounce as a future student at UWM. Go Panthers!

Coloring page illustrations created by Dana Coniff Breunig, '02.

PROUD PANTHER PAL

In recognition of the successful reading of the Hello, Pounce! book,

_____

is hereby named a Proud Panther Pal by the authority of the UWM Alumni Association.

Pounce Panther

Official UWM Mascot-in-Residence

UWM PROUD PANTHER

GO PANTHERS!

We are excited about your future.
Welcome to the University of Wisconsin-Milwaukee family!